EMBRACE YOUR BODY

PUFFIN BOOKS
UK | USA | Canada | Ireland | Australia
India | New Zealand | South Africa | China

 Penguin
Random House
Australia

Penguin Random House Australia is part of the Penguin Random House group of companies whose addresses can be found at global.penguinrandomhouse.com.

First published by Puffin Books, an imprint of Penguin Random House Australia Pty Ltd, in 2020

Printed and bound in China

 A catalogue record for this book is available from the National Library of Australia
NATIONAL LIBRARY OF AUSTRALIA

ISBN 978 1 760895 98 3 (Hardback)

Penguin Random House Australia uses papers that are natural and recyclable products, made from wood grown in sustainable forests. The logging and manufacture processes are expected to conform to the environmental regulations of the country of origin.

penguin.com.au

TARYN BRUMFITT

EMBRACE YOUR BODY

ILLUSTRATED BY SINEAD HANLEY

PUFFIN BOOKS

Some people in this world will tell you to look different.

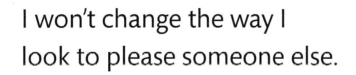

I won't change the way I
look to please someone else.

My body is unique, every body's different.

Look what my body can do.

I'm grateful for my eyes,
they see the world around me.

I'm grateful for my arms, to hug my family.

I'm grateful for my heart, filling me with kindness.

Listen to your **strong heartbeat**.

My body is my home, and what it does is magic.
My body keeps me strong, a vehicle to my dreams.

My beauty is inside, my beauty is my kindness.

We all know that kindness is key.

I'm gonna embrace my body,

I've only got one.

I'm gonna embrace my body,

show it some love.

Please don't compare me to someone else.
Embrace your body, everybody, love yourself.

Your body is somebody 'cause nobody's got a body like you.

Your body,

my body,

there's room for every body.

EMBRACE YOUR BODY!

Hi! I'm Taryn Brumfitt.

I'm the author of the book you are holding.
I'm also a mum of three children – Oliver, Cruz and
Mikaela – and founder of The Body Image Movement.
I work with people around the world, teaching them to
embrace their bodies.

Thanks for reading *Embrace Your Body*. I hope it's left you feeling inspired.

The book is based on the song, *Embrace*, which I co-wrote with award-winning
children's entertainment band Pevan and Sarah.
Listen to the song at bodyimagemovement.com/embrace.
But be warned – it's very catchy! We loved the ideas in the song so
much that I just had to create this book!

What's next?

I'm working on a documentary called *Embrace Kids* for kids just like you! Keep an eye
out for it. You can also visit me online at bodyimagemovement.com
but remember to check with an adult first.

And if you see me on the street, give me a big high five – okay?
Until then, keep embracing!

Taryn Brumfitt x